ALIEN INVASION: SPORTS EDITION

BUMP, SET, SPIKE:

A TOUGH CHOICE

by Josh Anderson & Gil Conrad
illustrated by Turner Lange

TORCH GRAPHIC PRESS

Published in the United States of America by Cherry Lake Publishing Group
Ann Arbor, Michigan
www.cherrylakepublishing.com

Reading Adviser: Beth Walker Gambro, MS, Ed., Reading Consultant, Yorkville, IL

Book Design: Book Buddy Media

Photo Credits: page 1: ©DigitalVision Vectors / Getty Images; page 7: ©Official Volley Ball Rules / Wikimedia; page 13: ©Ryan Pierse / Getty Images; page 27: ©Klaus Vedfelt / Getty Images; clipboard background: ©t_kimura/Getty Images; galaxy background: ©vi73777 / Getty Images; volleyball court background: ©Ronnie Chua / Shutterstock

Torch Graphic Press is an imprint of Cherry Lake Publishing Group.

Library of Congress Cataloging-in-Publication Data has been filed and is available at catalog.loc.gov

Cherry Lake Publishing Group would like to acknowledge the work of the Partnership for 21st Century Learning, a Network of Battelle for Kids. Please visit http://www.battelleforkids.org/networks/p21 for more information.

Printed in the United States of America
Corporate Graphics

TABLE OF CONTENTS

SHARICE GARDINER
SHARICE IS A VOLLEYBALL STAR WHO LOOKS FORWARD TO SHOWING OFF HER SKILLS. HER BUSY SCHEDULE MEANS SHE HAS SOME CHOICES TO MAKE.

FORBATH
FORBATH IS AN ALIEN FROM THE PLANET EXBERG. SHE PLAYS THE SPORT THREE-SKIFF, WHICH MAKES HER A MASTER MULTITASKER.

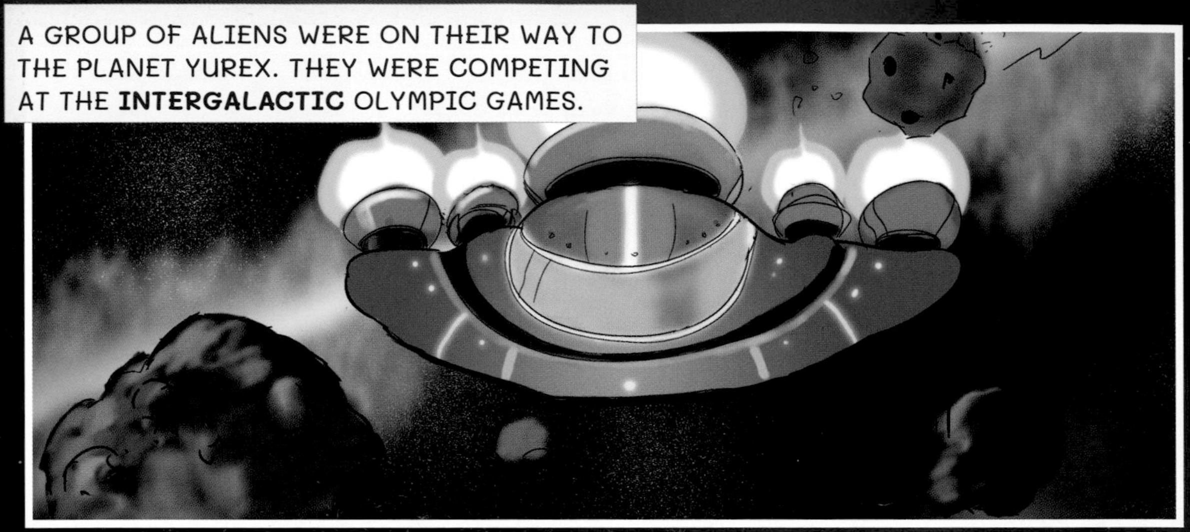
A GROUP OF ALIENS WERE ON THEIR WAY TO THE PLANET YUREX. THEY WERE COMPETING AT THE **INTERGALACTIC** OLYMPIC GAMES.

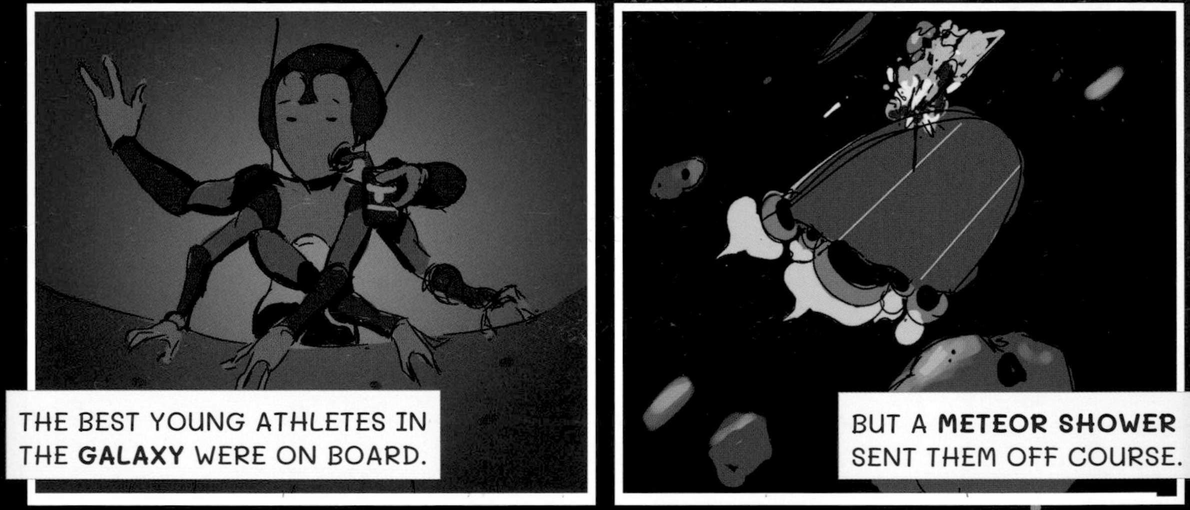
THE BEST YOUNG ATHLETES IN THE **GALAXY** WERE ON BOARD.
BUT A **METEOR SHOWER** SENT THEM OFF COURSE.

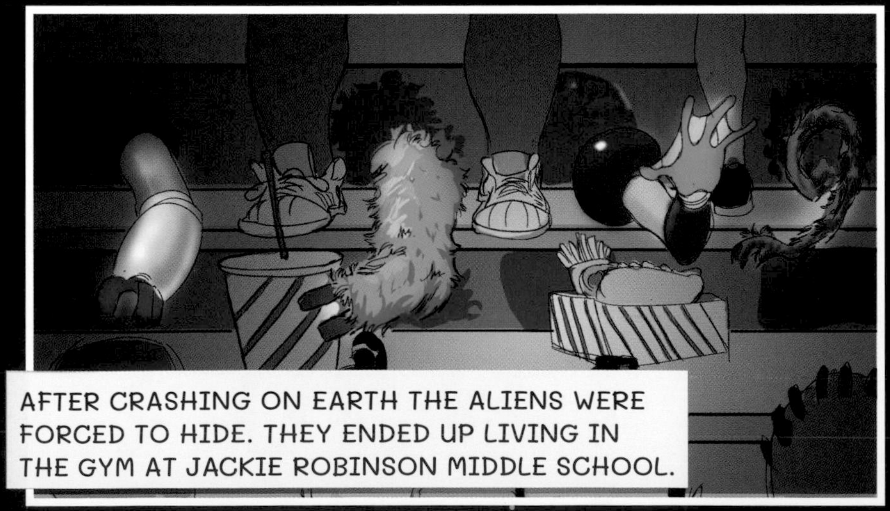
AFTER CRASHING ON EARTH THE ALIENS WERE FORCED TO HIDE. THEY ENDED UP LIVING IN THE GYM AT JACKIE ROBINSON MIDDLE SCHOOL.

intergalactic: between galaxies in space

galaxy: a system of stars and their solar systems

meteor shower: a group of space rocks that fall as they enter Earth's atmosphere

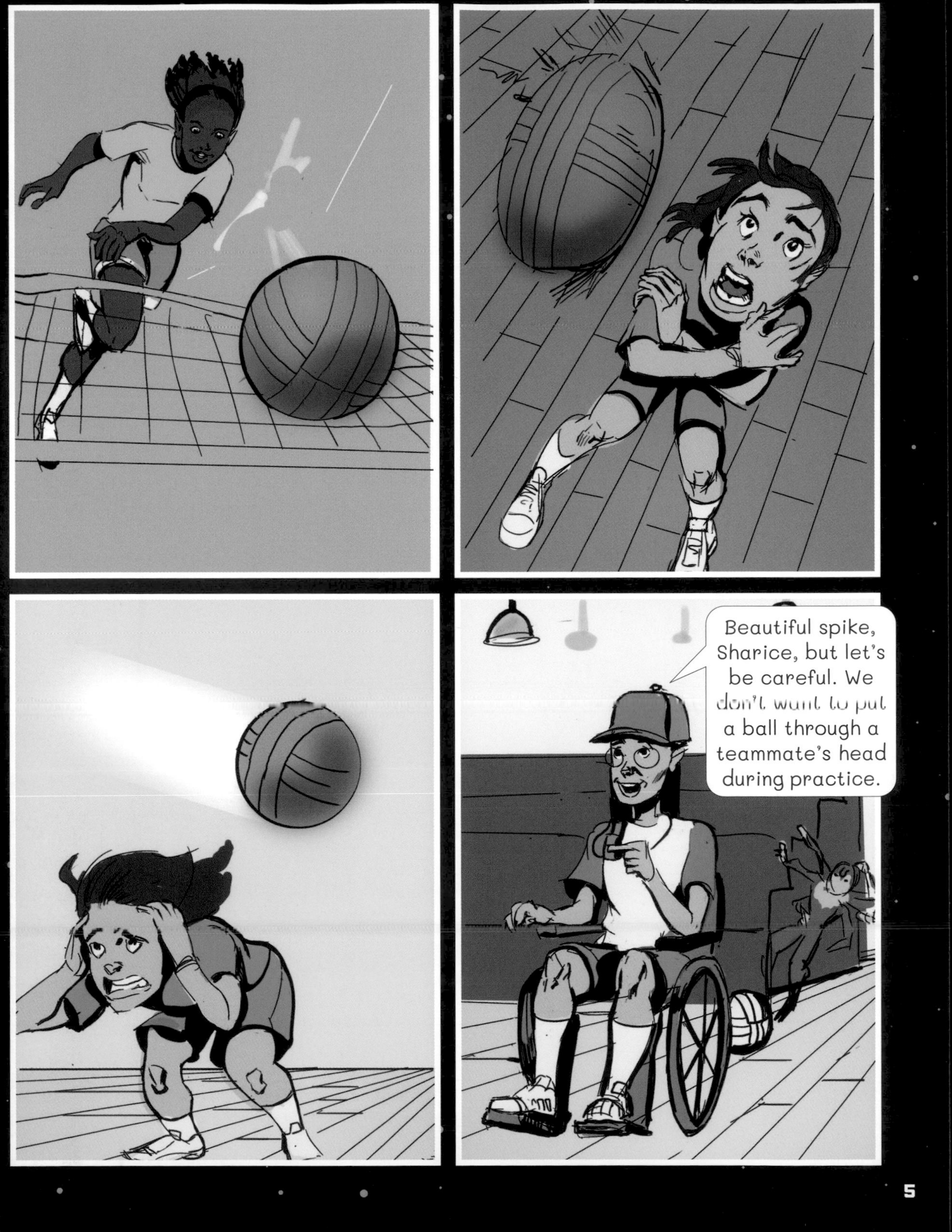
Beautiful spike, Sharice, but let's be careful. We don't want to put a ball through a teammate's head during practice.

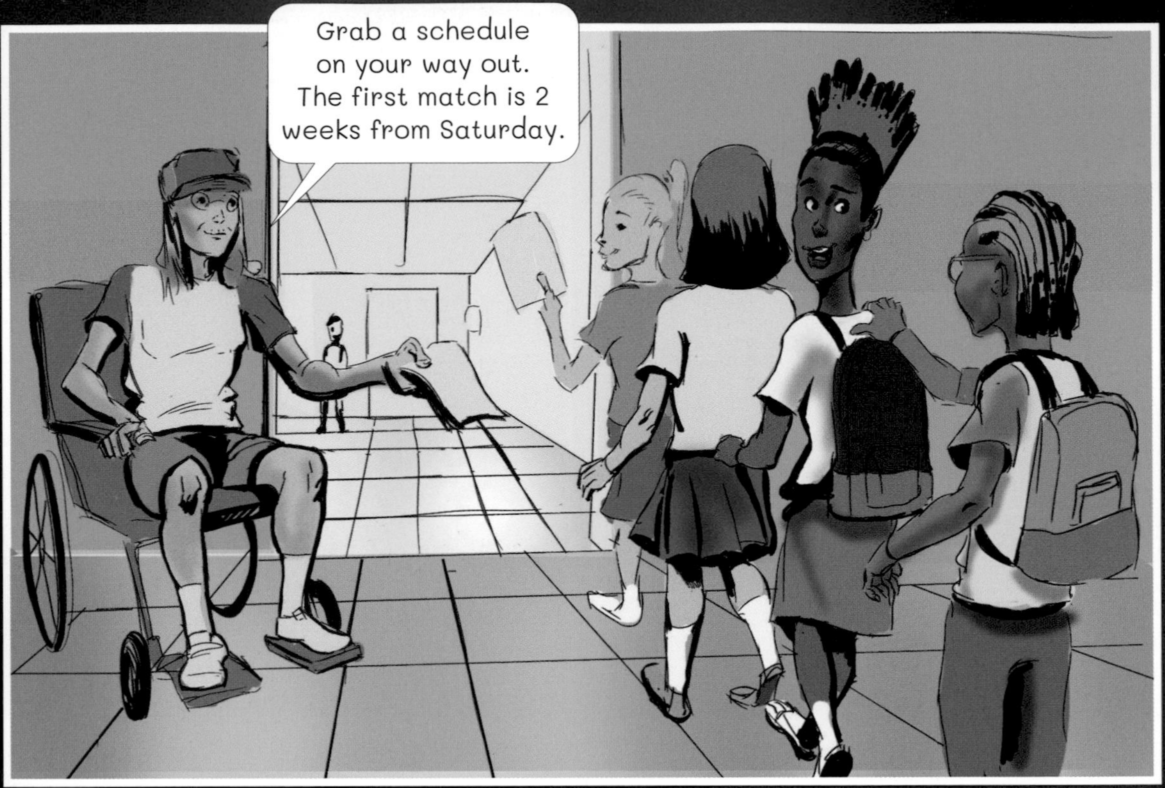
Grab a schedule on your way out. The first match is 2 weeks from Saturday.

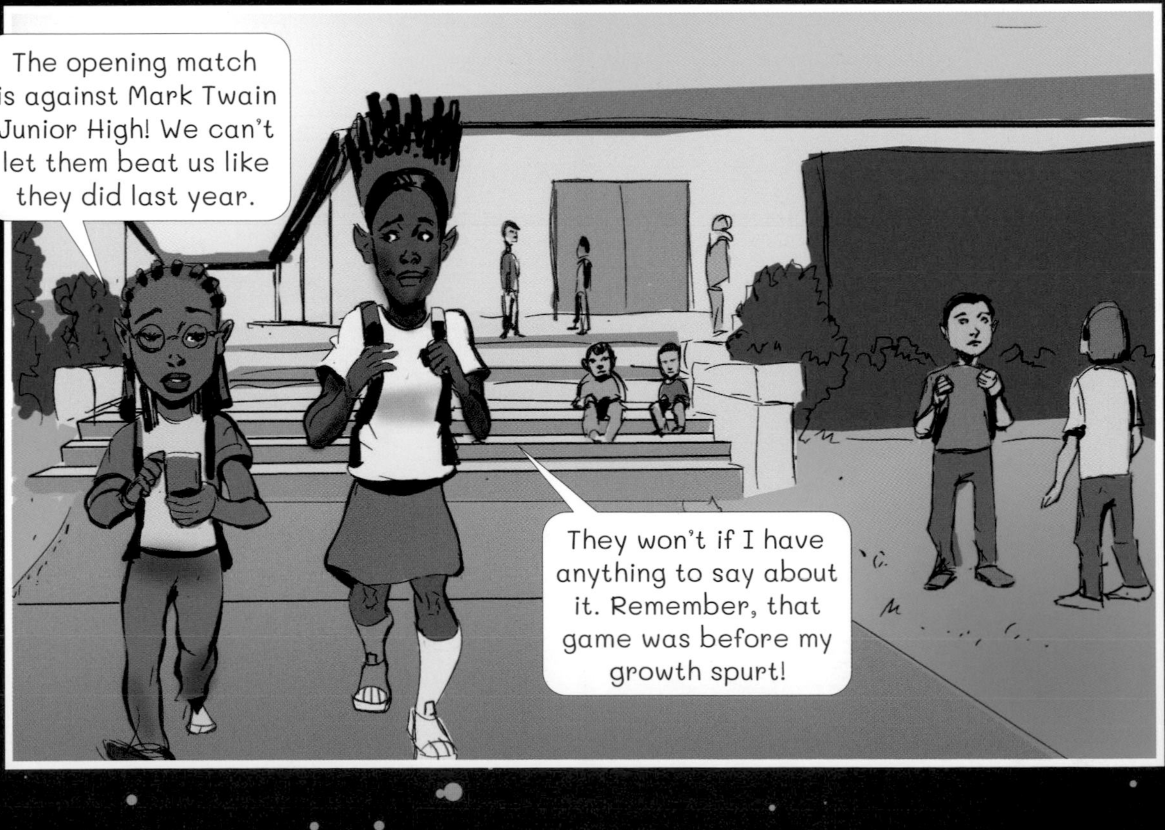
The opening match is against Mark Twain Junior High! We can't let them beat us like they did last year.
They won't if I have anything to say about it. Remember, that game was before my growth spurt!

HISTORY OF VOLLEYBALL

William G. Morgan invented volleyball in 1895. Basketball had been invented only 4 years earlier. Morgan was the physical education director at a YMCA. He created volleyball for older players who might feel basketball was too rough for them.

Volleyball was originally played with a shorter net and no limit to the number of players. Now, there are usually 6 players on each team. Beach volleyball was first played in 1915. In beach volleyball, each team has 2 players.

Volleyball was first played at the Tokyo Olympics in 1964. Beach volleyball was added to the Olympics in 1996.

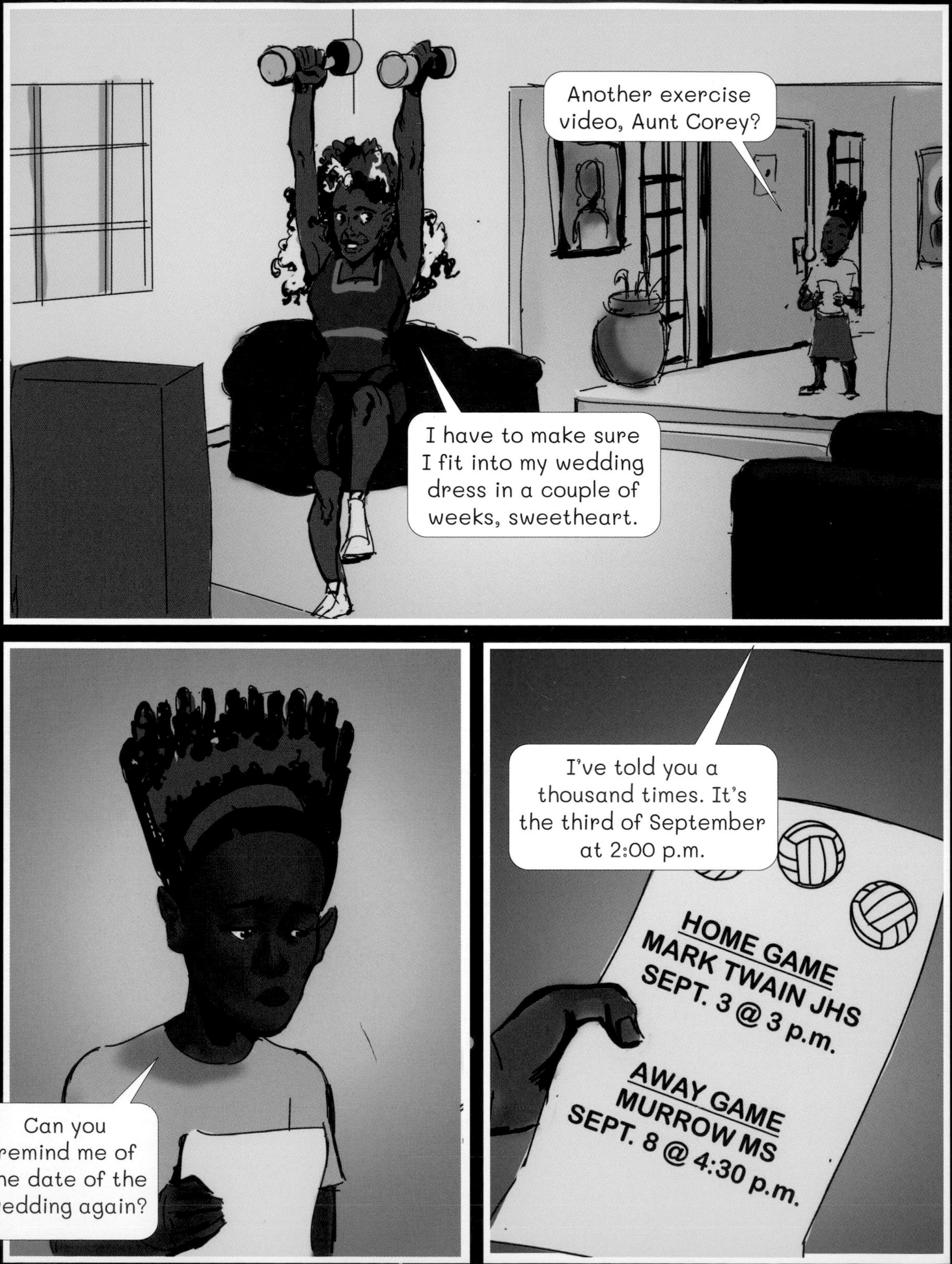

Another exercise video, Aunt Corey?
I have to make sure I fit into my wedding dress in a couple of weeks, sweetheart.
Can you remind me of the date of the wedding again?
I've told you a thousand times. It's the third of September at 2:00 p.m.
HOME GAME
MARK TWAIN JHS
SEPT. 3 @ 3 p.m.
AWAY GAME
MURROW MS
SEPT. 8 @ 4:30 p.m.

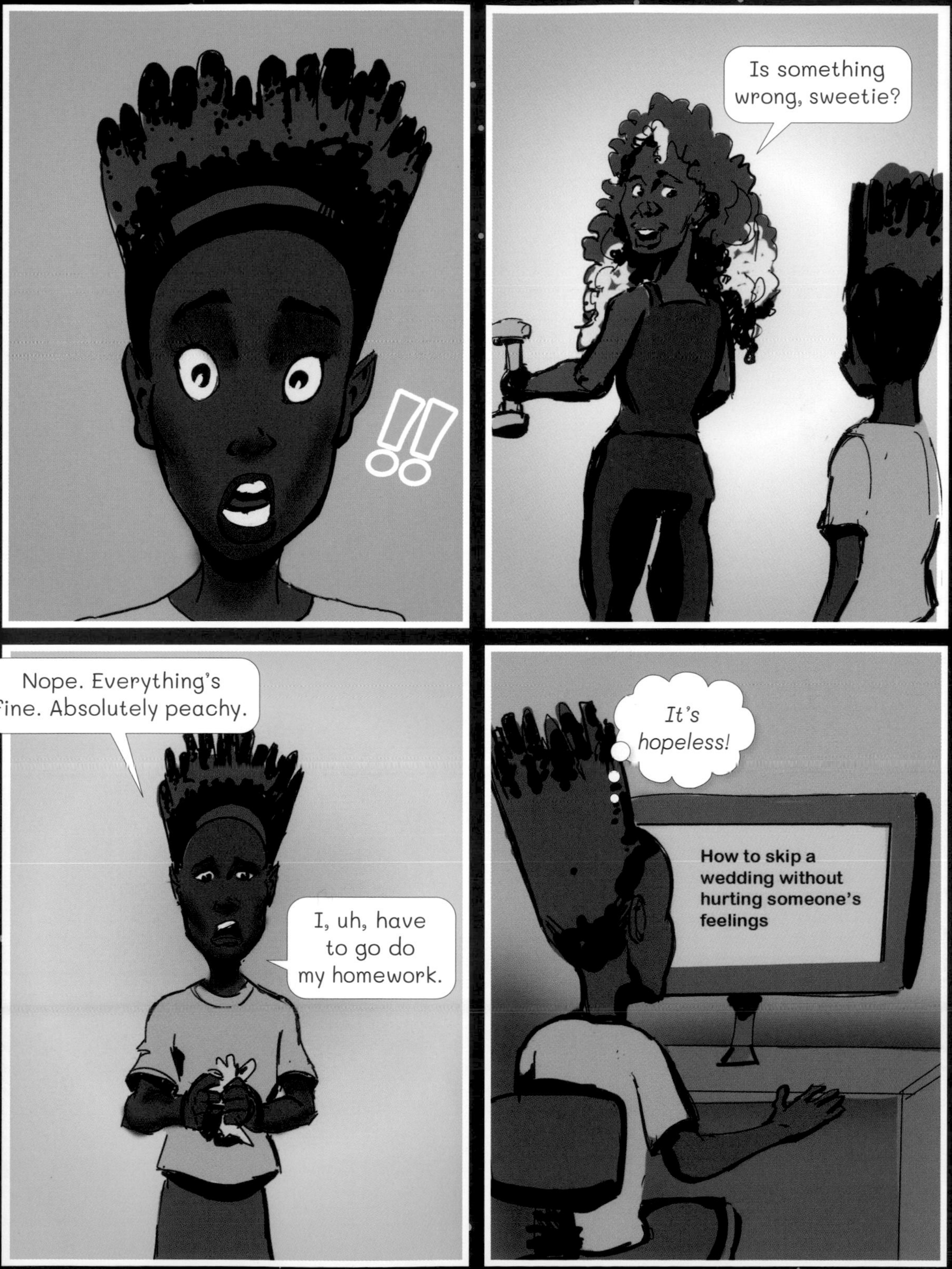
Is something wrong, sweetie?
Nope. Everything's fine. Absolutely peachy.
I, uh, have to go do my homework.
It's hopeless!
How to skip a wedding without hurting someone's feelings

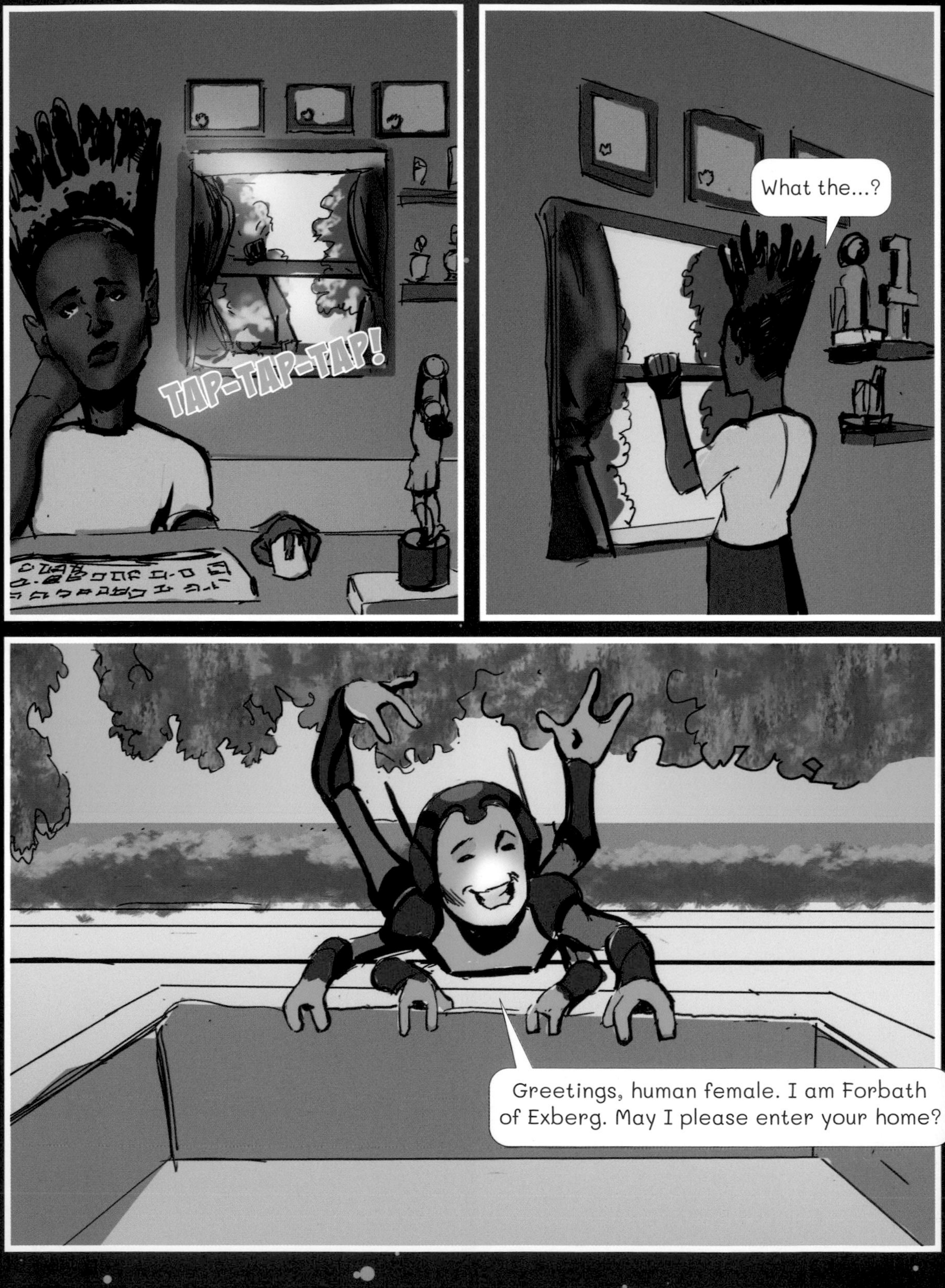
TAP-TAP-TAP!
What the...?
Greetings, human female. I am Forbath of Exberg. May I please enter your home?

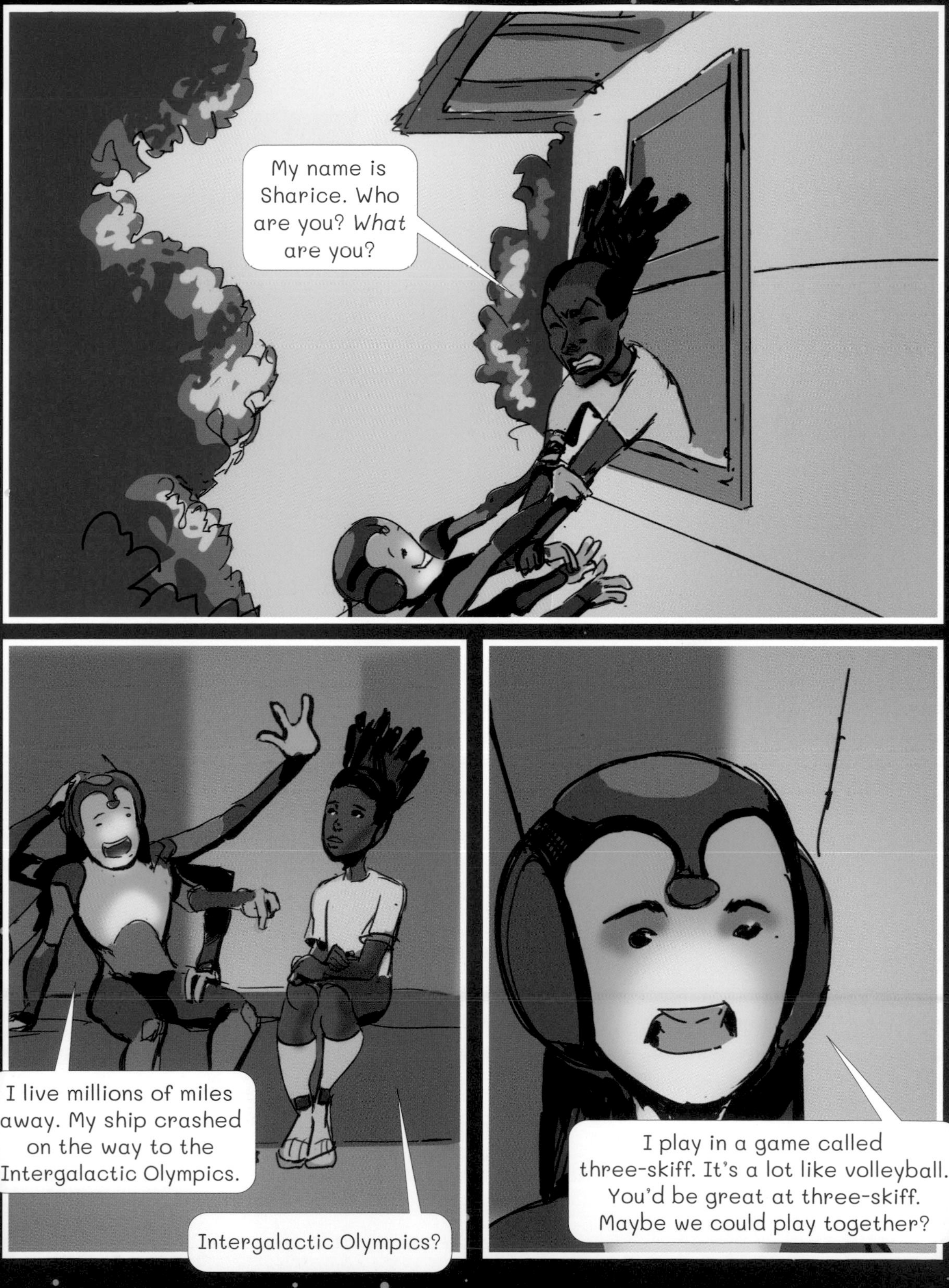
My name is Sharice. Who are you? *What* are you?
I live millions of miles away. My ship crashed on the way to the Intergalactic Olympics.
Intergalactic Olympics?
I play in a game called three-skiff. It's a lot like volleyball. You'd be great at three-skiff. Maybe we could play together?

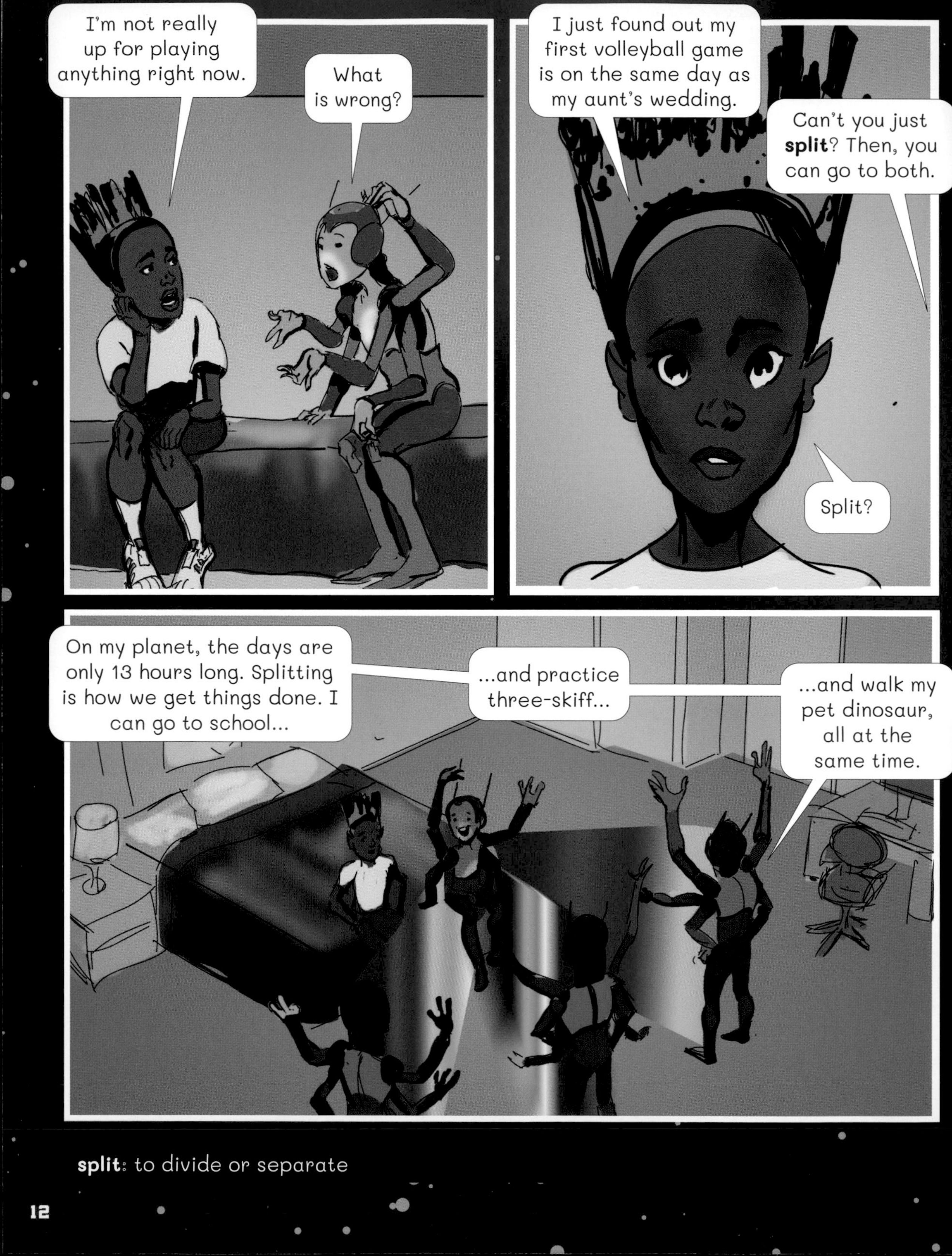
I'm not really up for playing anything right now.
What is wrong?
I just found out my first volleyball game is on the same day as my aunt's wedding.
Can't you just **split**? Then, you can go to both.
Split?
On my planet, the days are only 13 hours long. Splitting is how we get things done. I can go to school...
...and practice three-skiff...
...and walk my pet dinosaur, all at the same time.

split: to divide or separate

THE GOAT

Misty May-Treanor and Kerri Walsh Jennings are volleyball players. They are considered to be the greatest beach volleyball team ever to play the sport. They competed against each other in high school. It wasn't until after college in 2001 that they formed a team.

The pair earned 3 Olympic gold medals in 2004, 2008, and 2012. From August 2007 to August 2008, they won 112 matches in a row and 19 straight tournaments. The duo also took 3 World Championships together.

After retiring from the sport, Misty May-Treanor went on to coach volleyball. Kerri Walsh Jennings returned to the Olympics, but with a new partner.

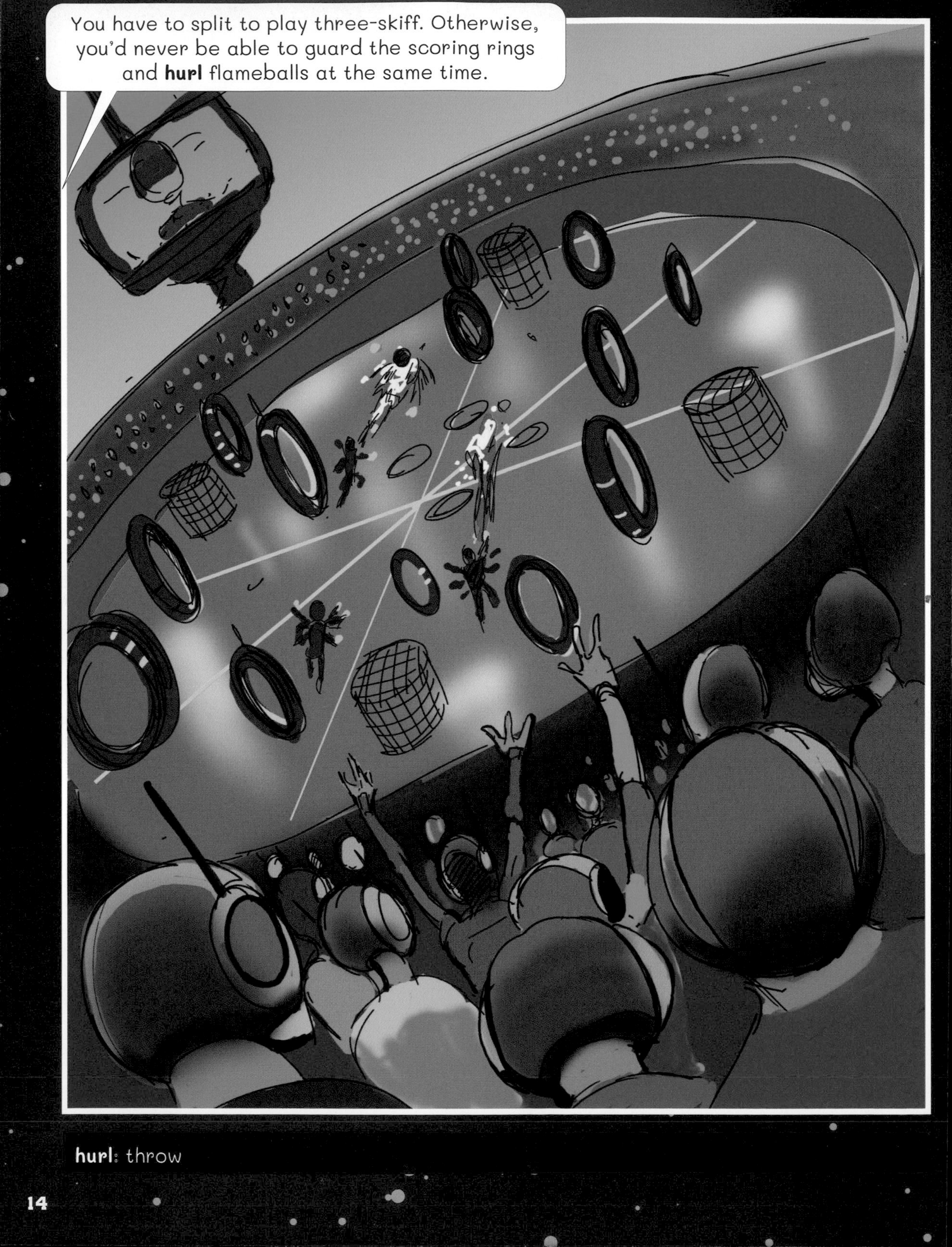
You have to split to play three-skiff. Otherwise, you'd never be able to guard the scoring rings and **hurl** flameballs at the same time.

hurl: throw

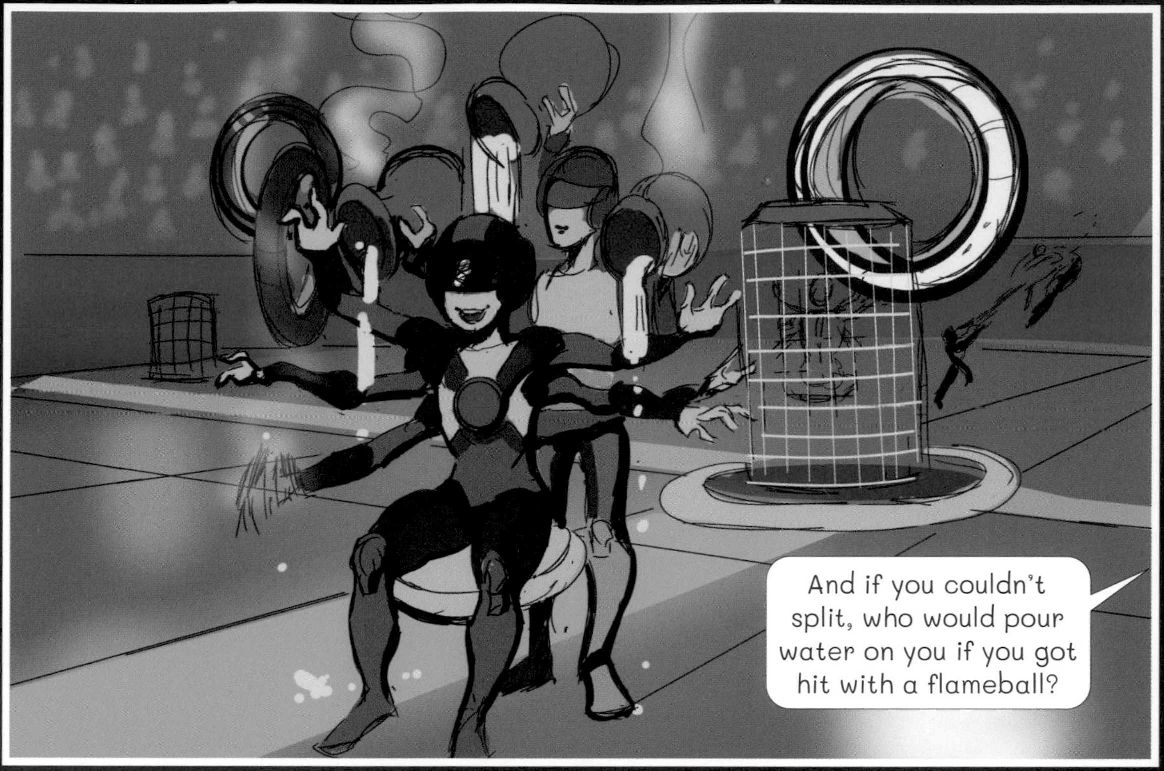
And if you couldn't split, who would pour water on you if you got hit with a flameball?

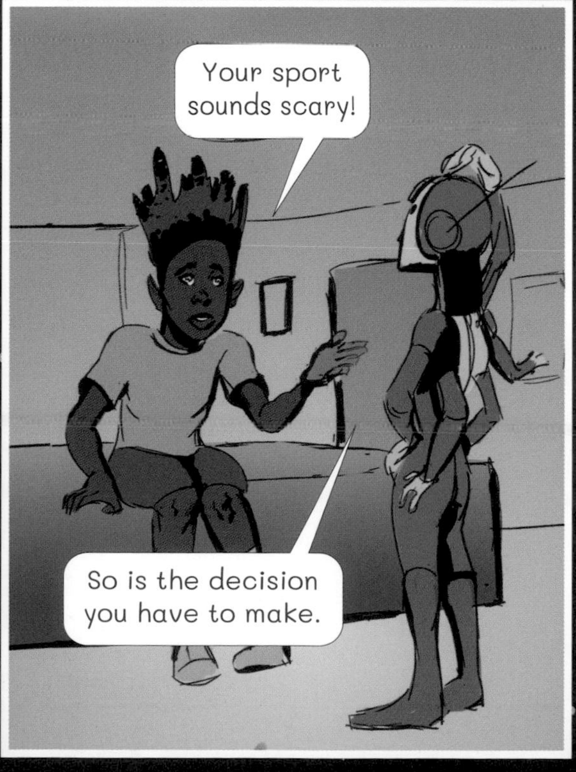
Your sport sounds scary!
So is the decision you have to make.

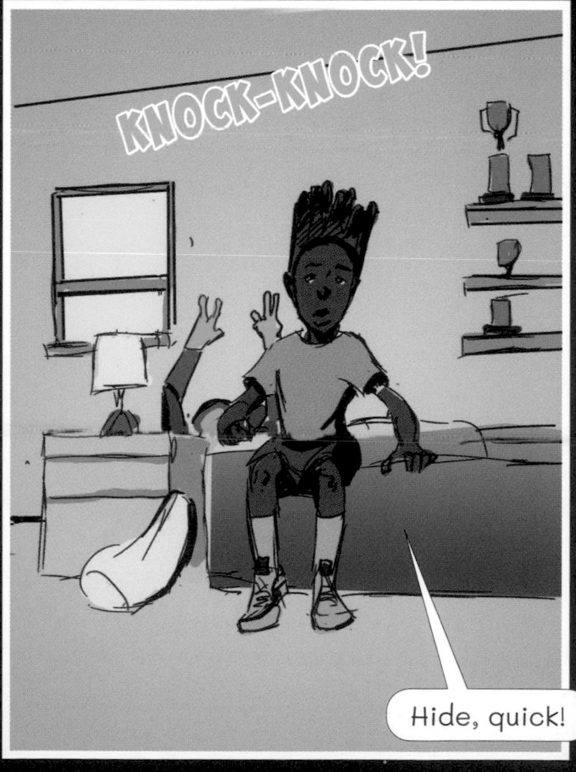
KNOCK-KNOCK!
Hide, quick!

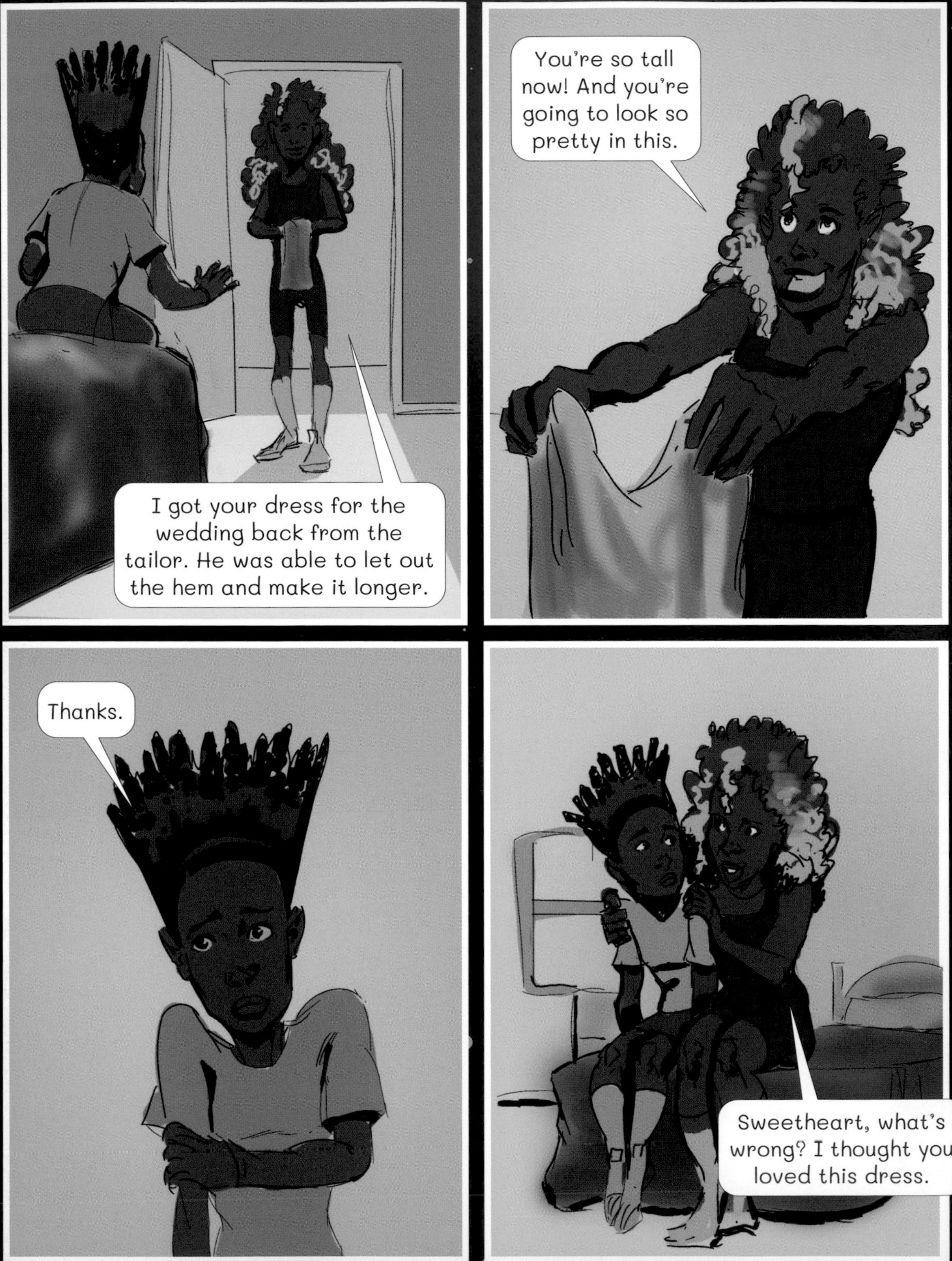
I got your dress for the wedding back from the tailor. He was able to let out the hem and make it longer.
You're so tall now! And you're going to look so pretty in this.
Thanks.
Sweetheart, what's wrong? I thought you loved this dress.

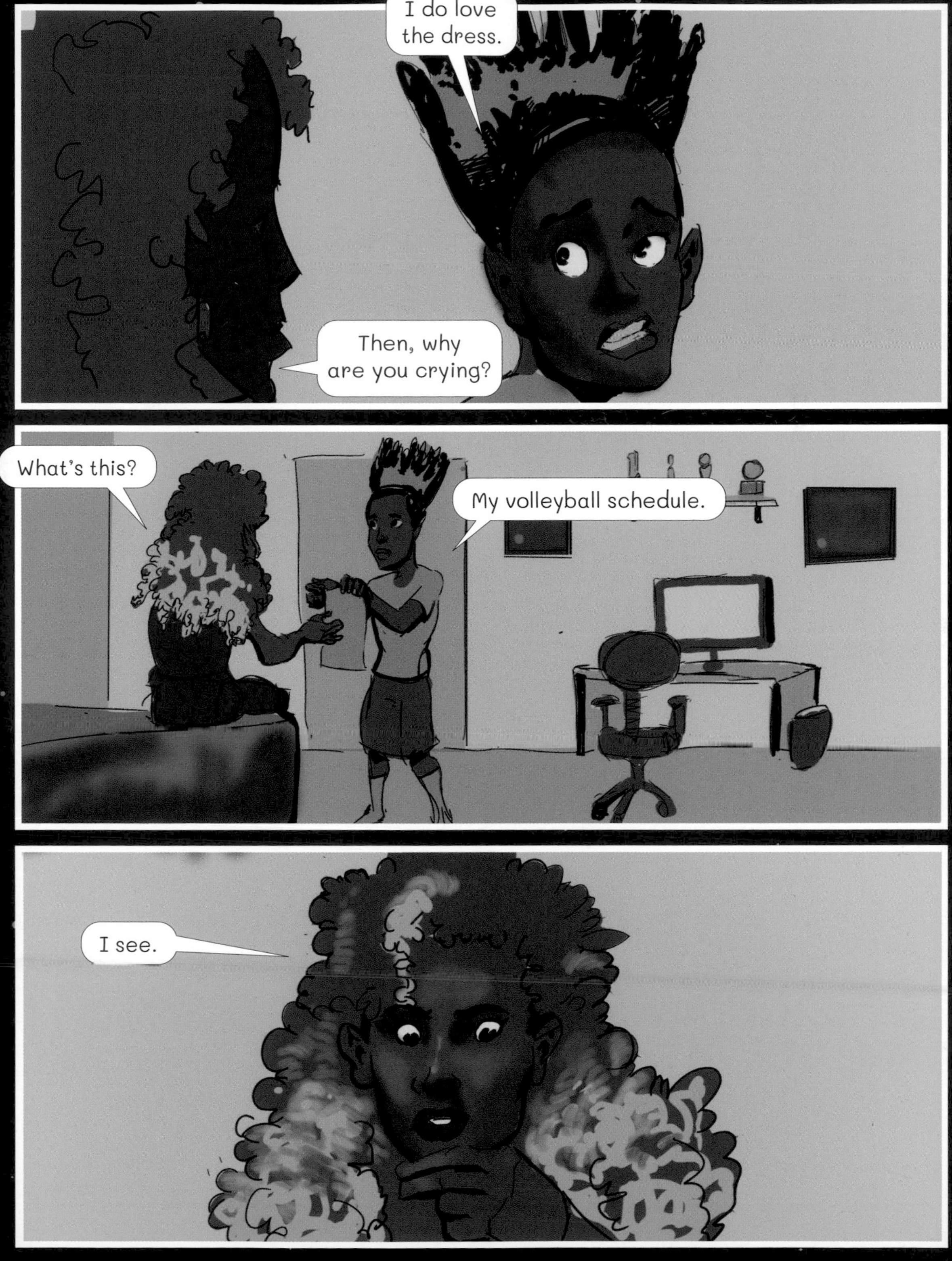
I do love the dress.
Then, why are you crying?
What's this?
My volleyball schedule.
I see.

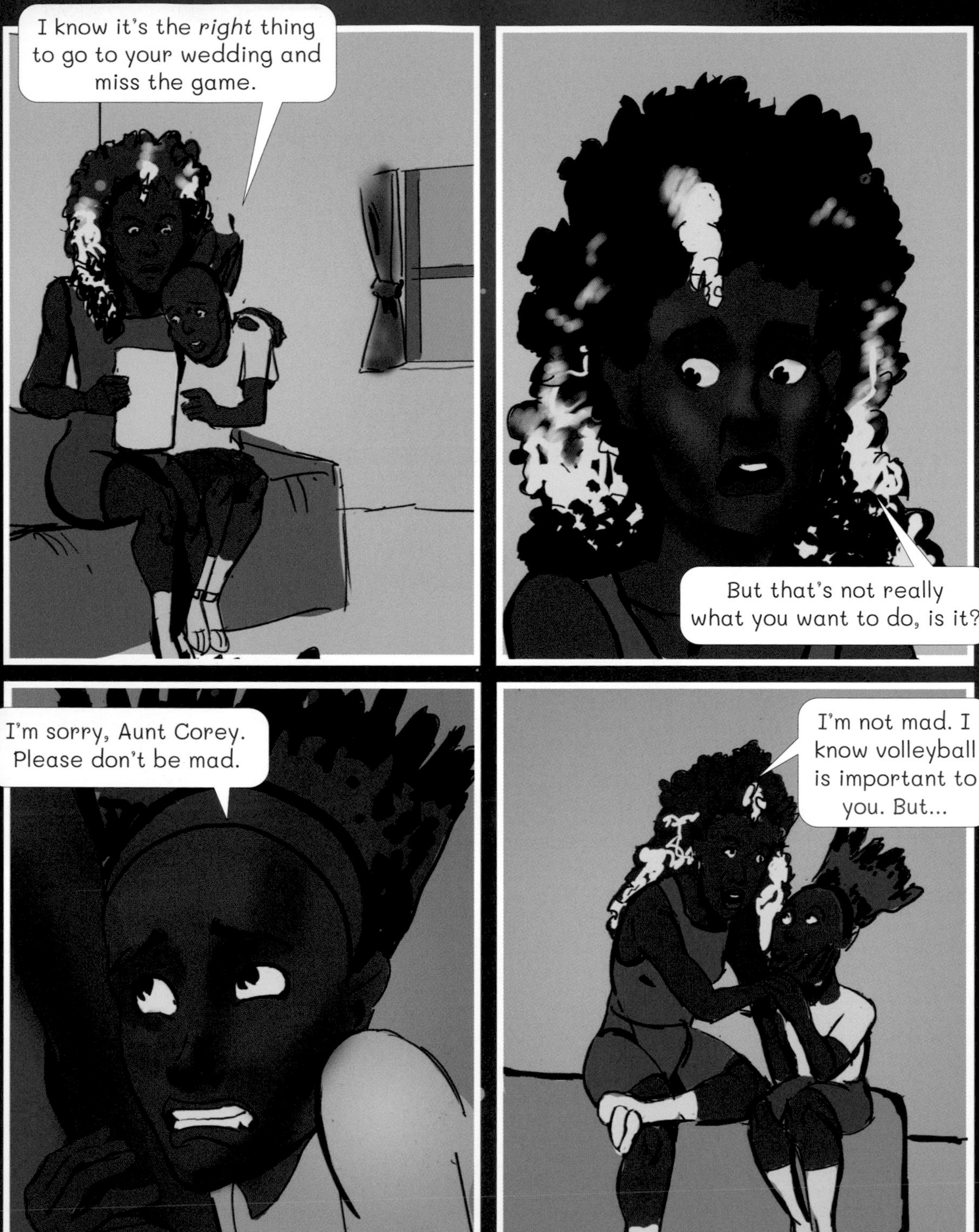
I know it's the *right* thing to go to your wedding and miss the game.
But that's not really what you want to do, is it?
I'm sorry, Aunt Corey. Please don't be mad.
I'm not mad. I know volleyball is important to you. But...

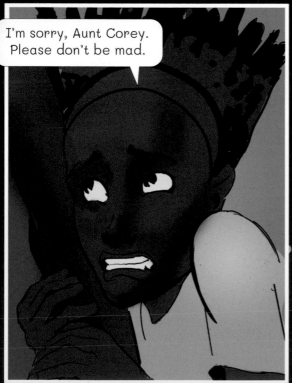

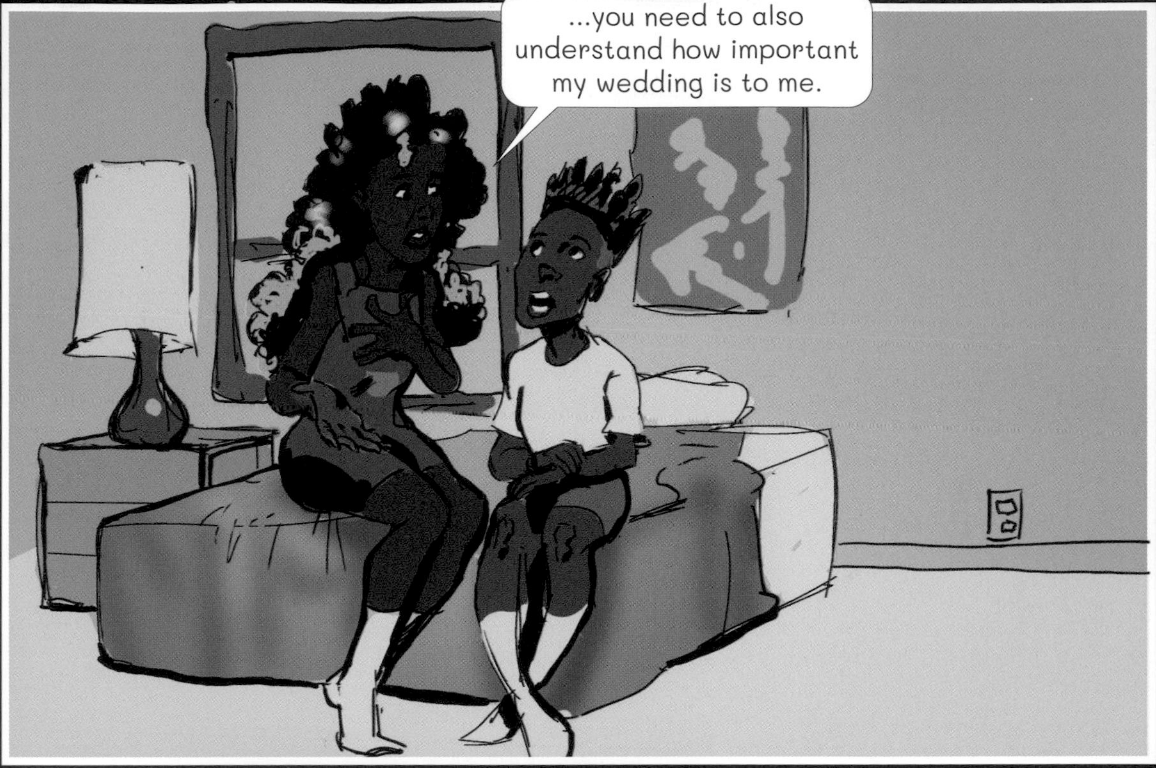
...you need to also understand how important my wedding is to me.

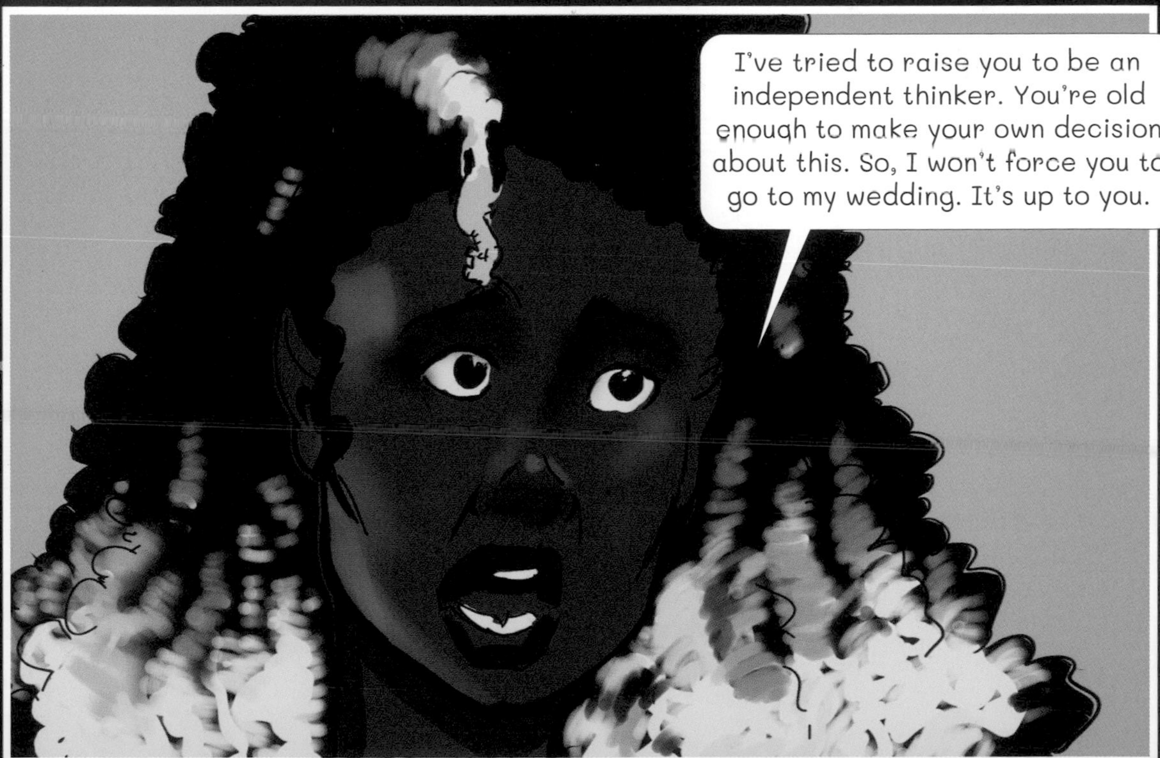
I've tried to raise you to be an independent thinker. You're old enough to make your own decision about this. So, I won't force you to go to my wedding. It's up to you.

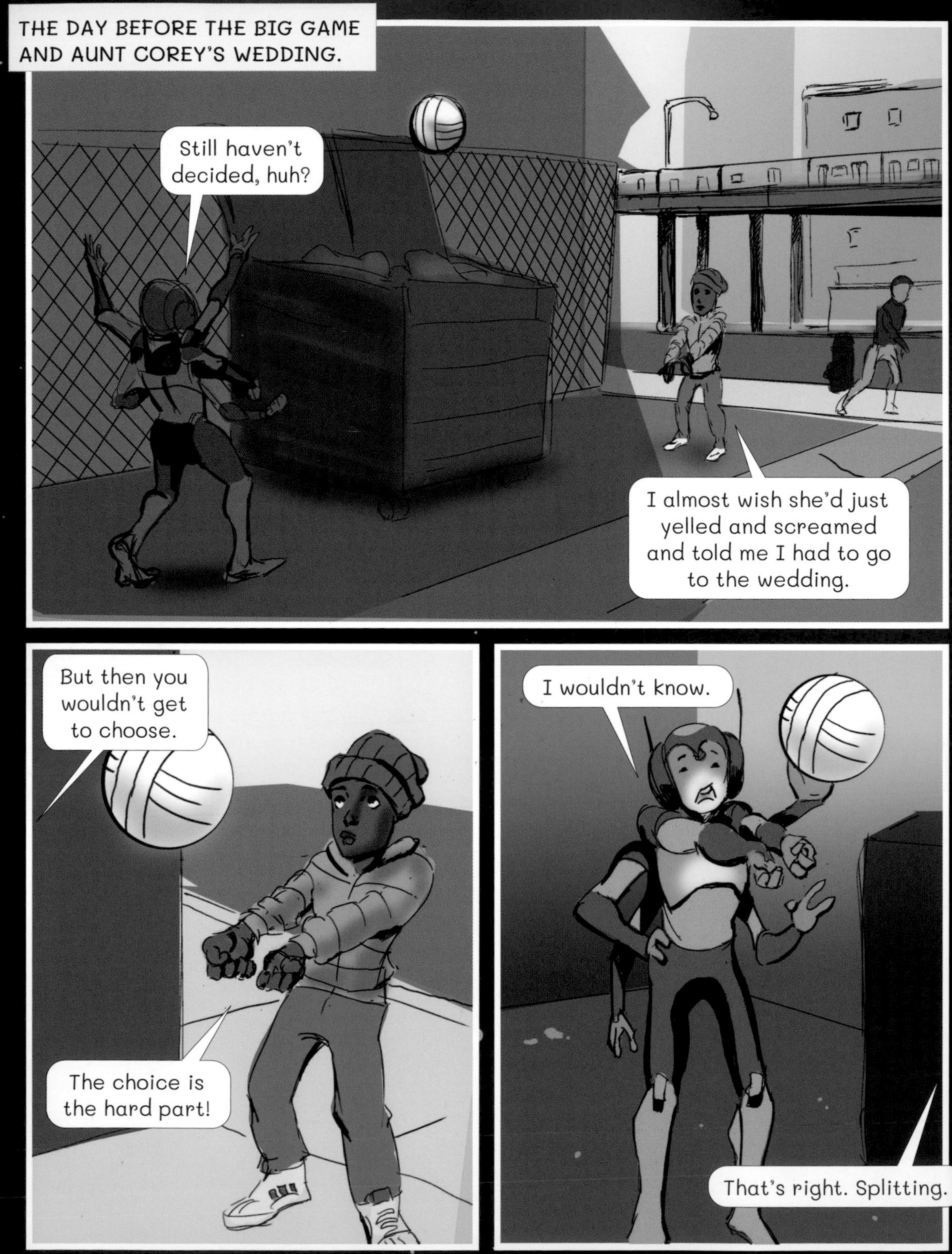
THE DAY BEFORE THE BIG GAME AND AUNT COREY'S WEDDING.
Still haven't decided, huh?
I almost wish she'd just yelled and screamed and told me I had to go to the wedding.
But then you wouldn't get to choose.
The choice is the hard part!
I wouldn't know.
That's right. Splitting.

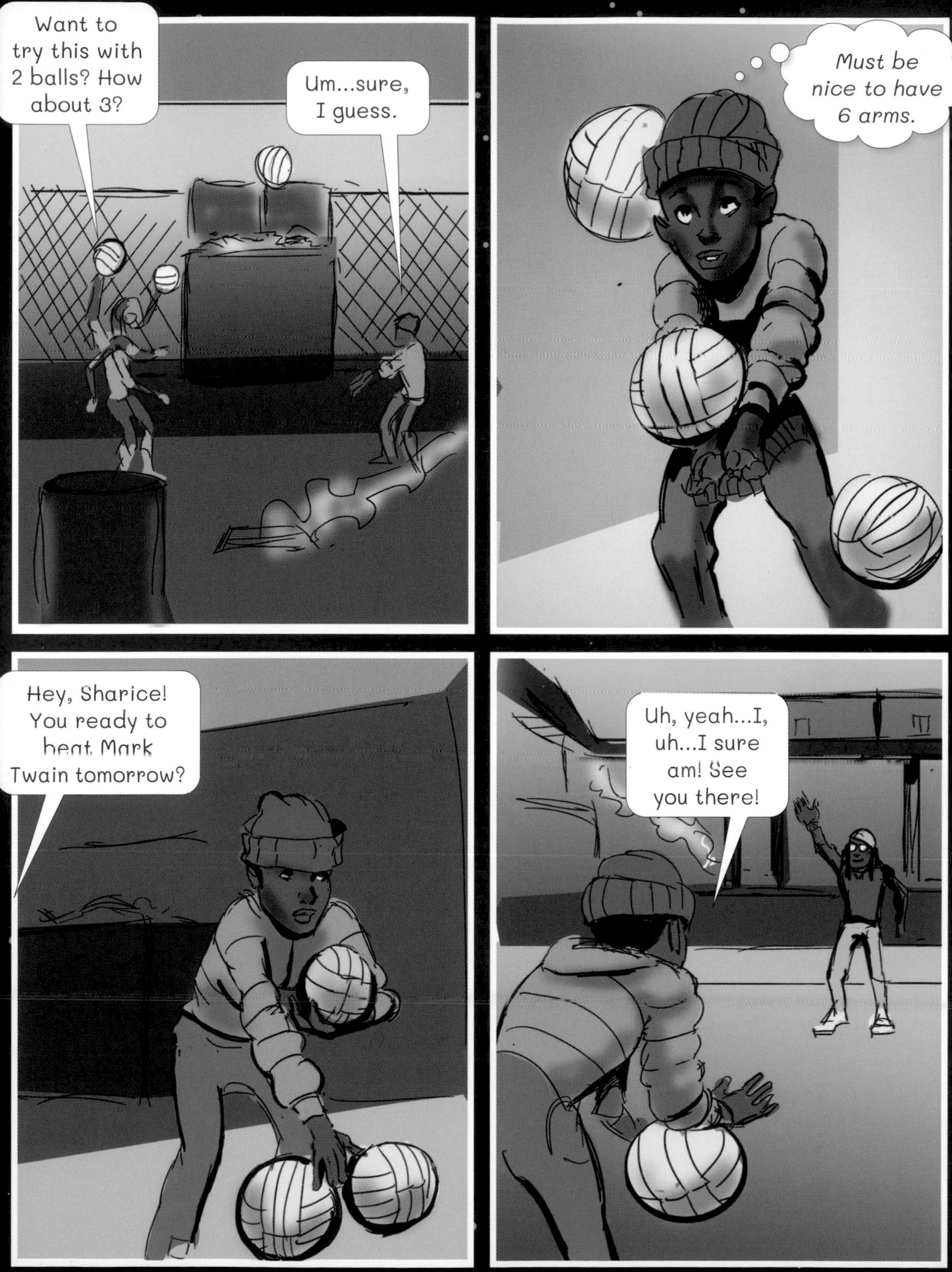

Want to try this with 2 balls? How about 3?
Um...sure, I guess.
Must be nice to have 6 arms.
Hey, Sharice! You ready to beat Mark Twain tomorrow?
Uh, yeah...I, uh...I sure am! See you there!

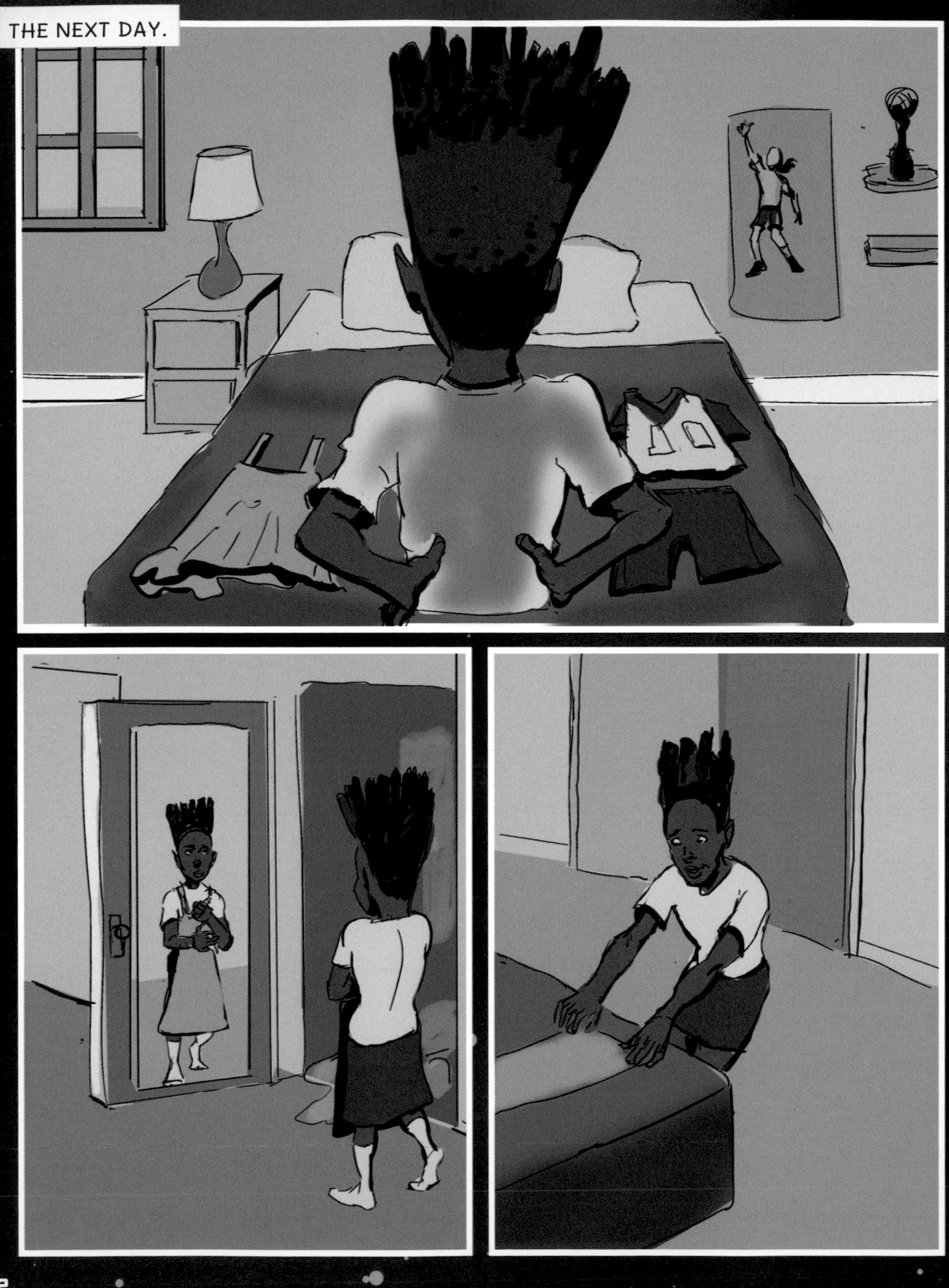
THE NEXT DAY.

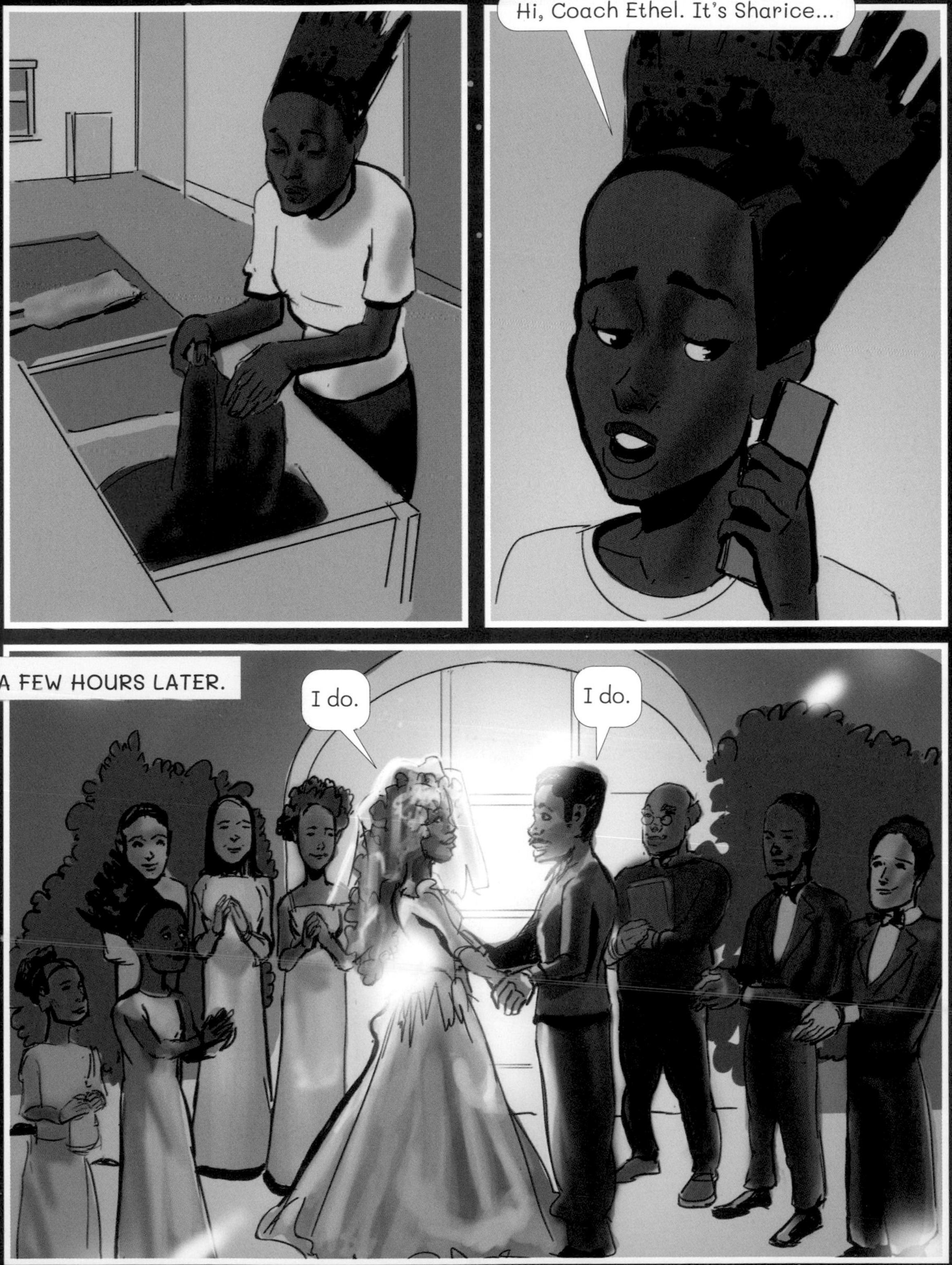
Hi, Coach Ethel. It's Sharice...
A FEW HOURS LATER.
I do.
I do.

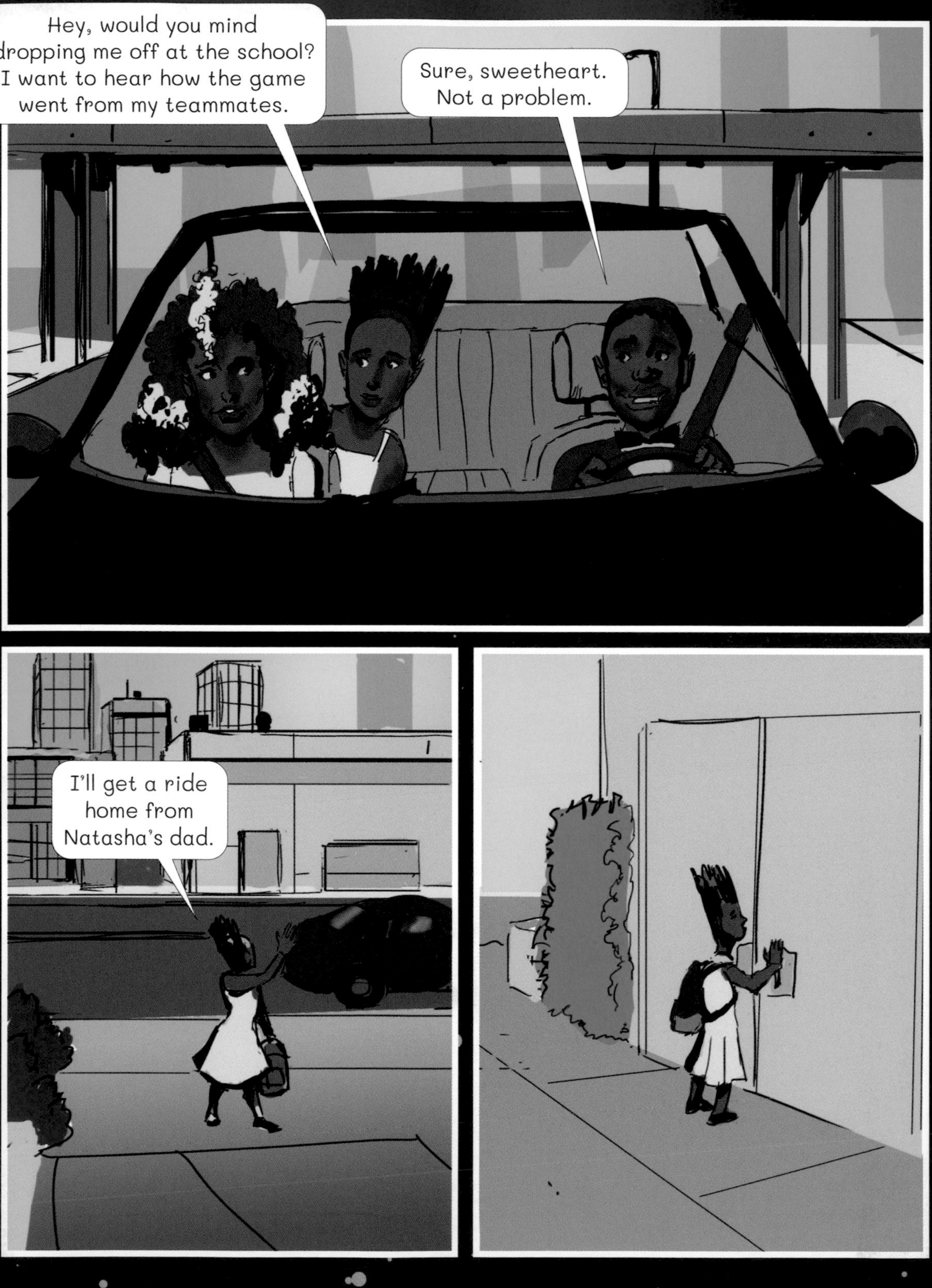
Hey, would you mind dropping me off at the school? I want to hear how the game went from my teammates.
Sure, sweetheart. Not a problem.
I'll get a ride home from Natasha's dad.

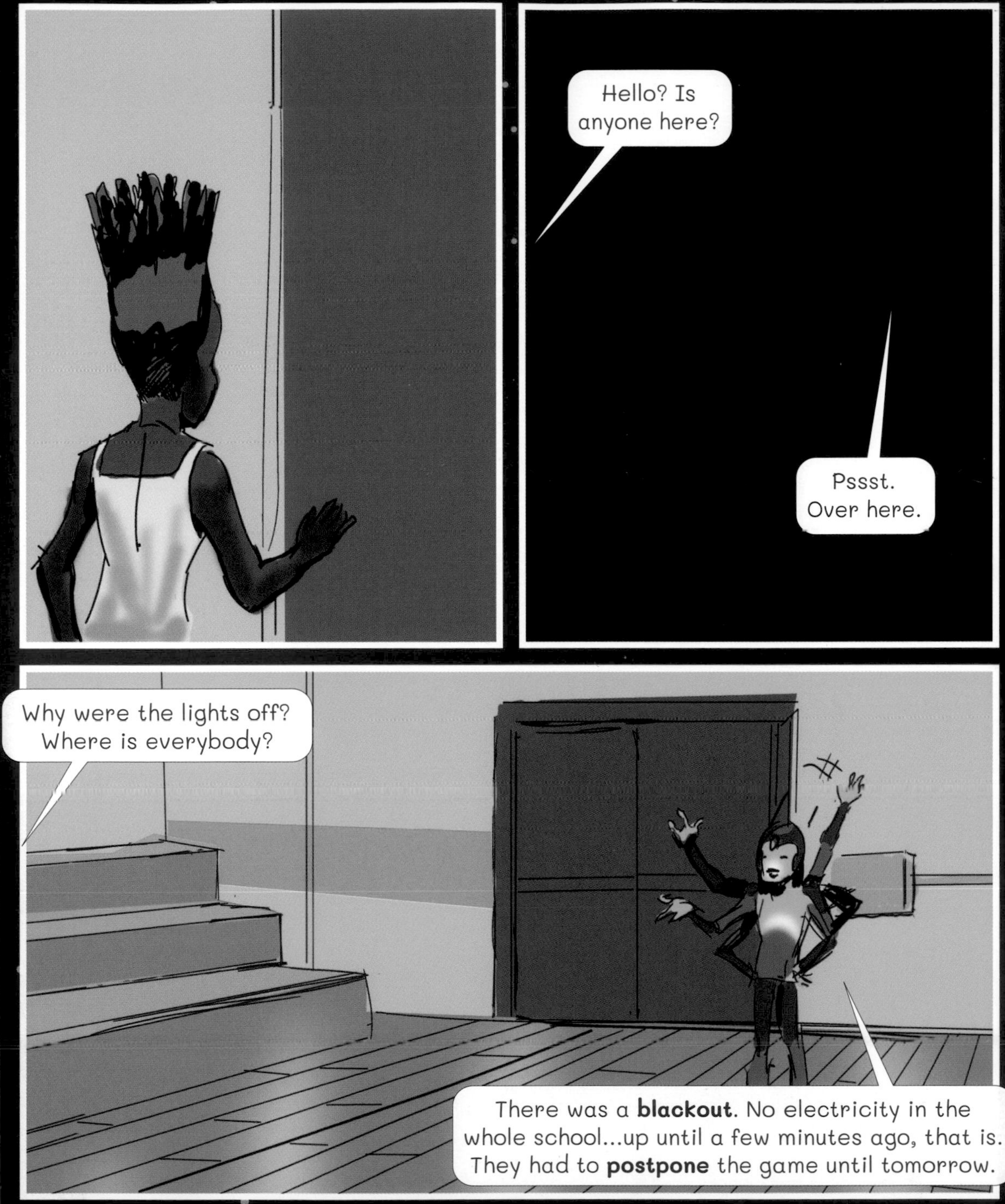
Hello? Is anyone here?
Pssst. Over here.
Why were the lights off? Where is everybody?
There was a **blackout**. No electricity in the whole school...up until a few minutes ago, that is. They had to **postpone** the game until tomorrow.

blackout: a loss of electrical power

postpone: to cause something to take place later than its original time

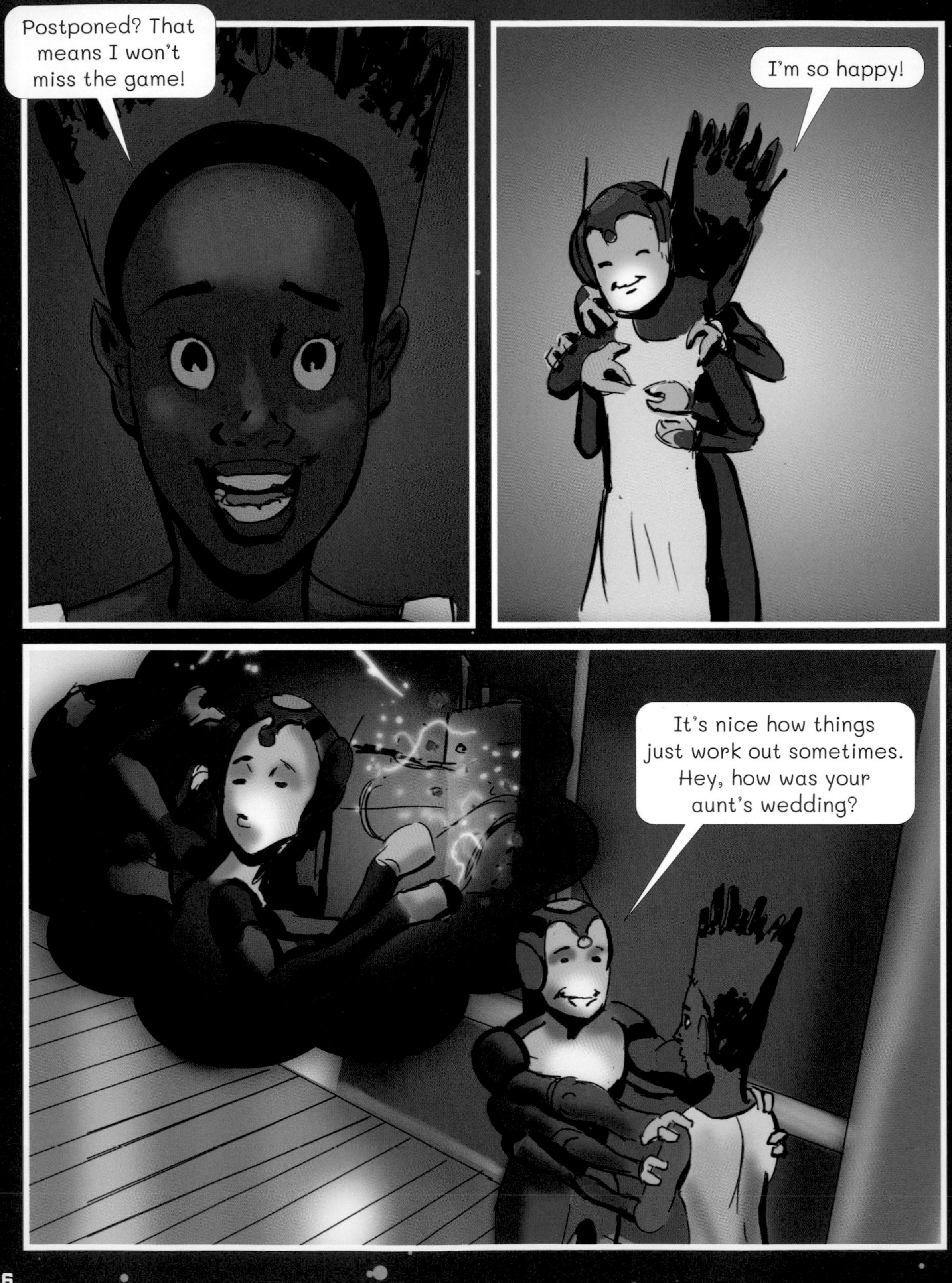
Postponed? That means I won't miss the game!
I'm so happy!
It's nice how things just work out sometimes. Hey, how was your aunt's wedding?

TOUGH DECISIONS

For kids and adults, every day is filled with choices. Some choices are small and might not matter much. Other choices are big and could have a large impact on your life. Taking the time to make good decisions is a very important life skill.

Big decisions can be scary. The first thing to do is identify the problem. Then, gather any important information to help make your choice. Spend some time thinking about all of the possible choices or solutions available. Remember that each choice has a consequence. After you have settled on what to do, it's time to take action!

Later, take some time to think back on your choice. Was it the right one? Even if it wasn't, you'll learn for the next time.

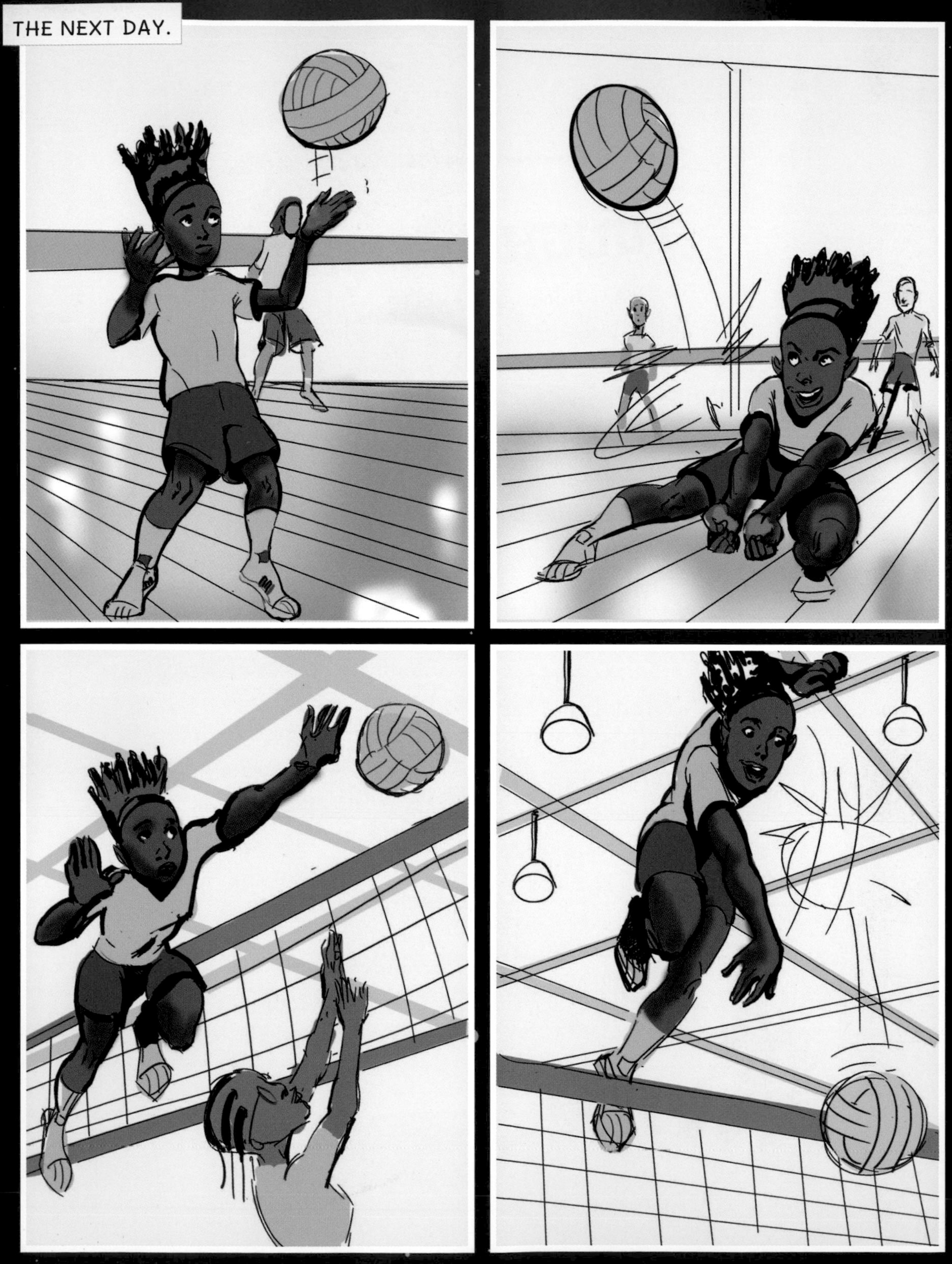
THE NEXT DAY.

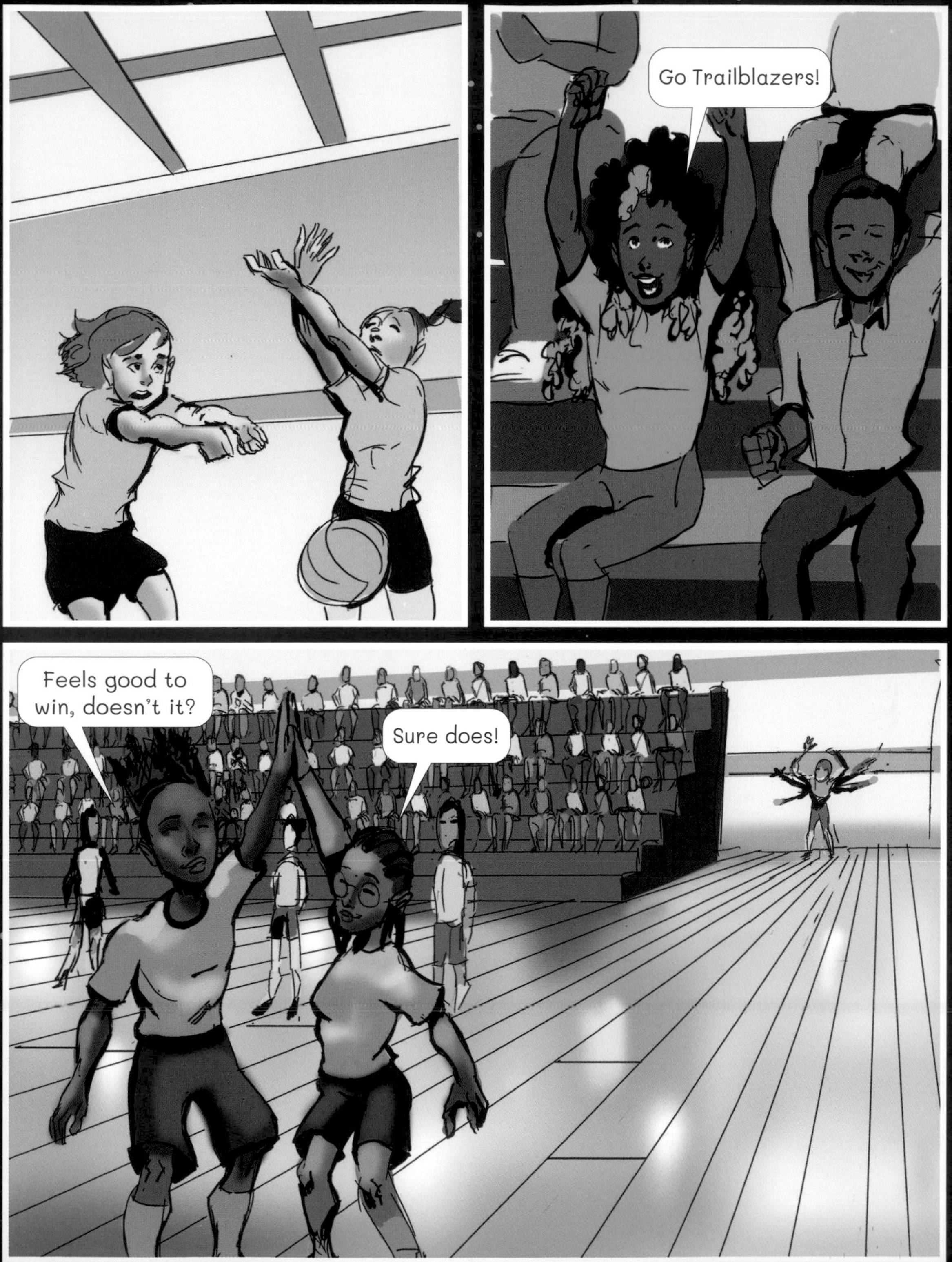
Go Trailblazers!
Feels good to win, doesn't it?
Sure does!

WOULD YOU RATHER?

Not all decisions have to be hard ones! Sometimes, a game can help teach you what's most important to you!

What You Need

* index cards

* 2 players

* pen

Steps to Take

1. Each player gets 10 index cards.

2. Each player writes 5 "happy activity" cards. These are activities you enjoy doing (things like "taking a long walk" and "going to watch a ball game"). Make a pile with both players' cards.

3. Each player writes 5 "unpleasant activity" cards. These are activities you might not enjoy as much (things like "taking out the trash" or "cleaning my room"). Make a second pile with both players' unpleasant activity cards.

4. Shuffle each pile.

5. Take turns flipping over 2 cards from either pile. Discuss.

LEARN MORE

BOOKS

Rule, Heather. *Olympic Games Upsets.* Minneapolis, MN: Lerner Publications, 2020.

Scheff, Matt. *The Summer Olympics: World's Best Athletic Competition.* Minneapolis, MN: Lerner Publications, 2021.

WEBSITES

Kiddle: Volleyball Facts for Kids
https://kids.kiddle.co/Volleyball

Olympic Games
https://www.olympic.org/volleyball

ALIEN CHARACTERS

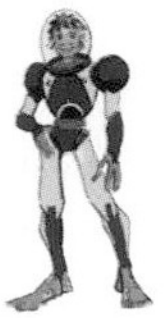

DARNEX
DARNEX IS A HETHITE FROM THE PLANET HETHA. ON HIS HOME PLANET, HE PLAYS THE SPORT WAVE RIDER. HIS BODY MAKES A STICKY GOO THAT SMELLS LIKE PINEAPPLE.

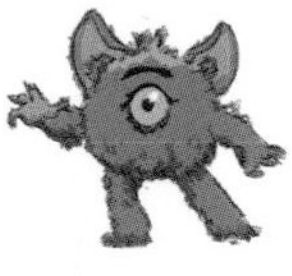

ZANG
ZANG IS AN ALIEN FROM PLANET SMONGTHURP. HE IS A PRO AT THE SPORT FLONGLOG, AND A PRO AT SIGN LANGUAGE.

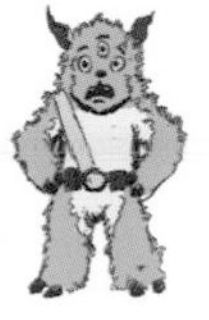

SPLART
SPLART IS AN ALIEN FROM THE PLANET TRASPEN. HE LOVES EATING BACON AND BASEBALLS. HE PLAYS SWAZBUL. IMAGINING FLOWERS AND SANDWICHES HELPS HIM RELAX.

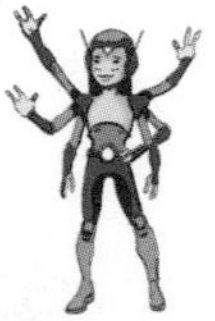

FORBATH
FORBATH IS AN ALIEN FROM THE PLANET EXBERG. SHE PLAYS THE SPORT THREE-SKIFF, WHICH MAKES HER A MASTER MULTITASKER.

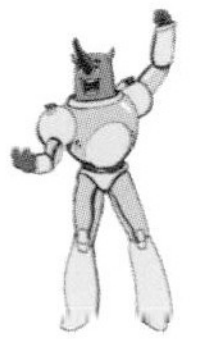

MIKKI
MIKKI IS AN ALIEN FROM PLANET KOPITER. HIS SPORT IS CRILLETTE. HE HAS WORKED HARD TO KEEP HIS COOL UNDER PRESSURE.

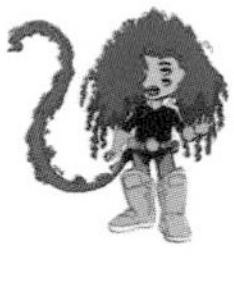

BOLI
BOLI IS AN ALIEN FROM THE PLANET OOH. SHE PLAYS THE TEAM SPORT ZINGER. SHE IS A GREAT TEAMMATE AND FRIEND TO EVERYONE.

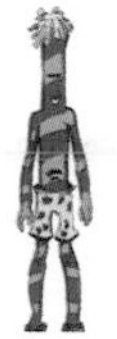

GAMEE GLAP
GAMEE IS AN ALIEN FROM THE PLANET MOOBSTRUM. HE IS A FLARFELL DIVE STAR. HE KNOWS HOW TO HANDLE BULLIES.

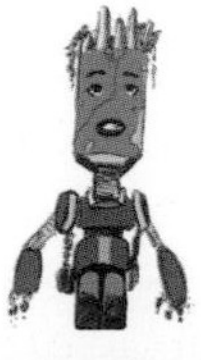

DREEPY
DREEPY IS AN INTERGALACTIC SPORTS STAR, AND SHE KNOWS IT. HER PLANET VALUES HONESTY OVER EVERYTHING. WHO WANTS TO GET SQUASHED BY A TRUTHY BOOT?

GLOSSARY

blackout (BLAK-owt) a loss of electrical power

galaxy (GAL-uk-see) a system of stars and their solar systems

hurl (HERL) throw

intergalactic (in-tuhr-guh-LAK-tik) between galaxies in space

meteor shower (MEE-tee-uhr SHOW-uhr) a group of space rocks that fall as they enter Earth's atmosphere

postpone (POST-pohn) to cause something to take place later than its original time

split (SPLIT) to divide or separate

INDEX